Dedication

This book is dedicated to leaders everywhere…Grandparents, Mothers, Fathers, Sisters, Brothers, Aunts, Uncles, Nieces, Nephews, Cousins, Friends, Educators and Professionals in every field! I would also like to dedicate this book to everyone who has influenced and led me in the right direction along my journey. Thank you all for being Transformational Leaders! *KLR*

Copyright © 2015 by Keichea L. Reever

All rights reserved. No part of this book may be reproduced, stored in a retrieval system, or transmitted in any form or by any means, electronic, mechanical, photocopying, recording, or otherwise, except as permitted by obtaining written permission from the publisher/author.

Published by the Southern California Mentoring Academy.
www.socalmentoringacademy.org

For more information, log on to our website above or call 562-506-0287. We can also be reached via email at info@socalmentoringacademy.org.

Manufactured in the United States of America.

ISBN: 0996128301
ISBN 13: 978-0-996-1283-0-8

Leading People

A Pathway to Personal Development

Keichea L. Reever, Ed.D.

Leading People: A Pathway to Personal Development

The Youth Citizenship Seminar (YCS) was created to increase each youth participant's leadership skills. MacNeil (2006) defines leadership as "a relational process combining ability (knowledge, skills, and talents) with authority (voice, influence, and decision-making power) to positively influence and impact diverse individuals, organizations, and communities" (p. 29). This definition of leadership combines the great man theories that were popular in the 1900's with the more modern trend in leadership theories that involves relationships between and amongst leaders and their followers. MacNeil extensively reviewed both popular and scholarly literature written on leadership theory, leadership development and leadership practice and stated that "youth are noticeably absent" (p. 29). She noted that "where young people are referenced, it is frequently with a future orientation. That is, the focus is on the need to begin working with young people now so they can develop the skills they will need to be effective leaders later" (p. 30).

"Youth leadership development is relatively new as an area of study" (Libby et al., 2006, p.16). In addition, programs that have promoted youth leadership development in the past "have often been seen as character development, life preparation, and contributing to building relationships and community" (Libby et al., p. 16). Similar to the literature written on adult leadership theory, leadership development and leadership practice "the field of youth development, and the increasing body of research in the field, has also contributed to arguments for the need of youth leadership development, often emphasizing how those learning experiences might be structured, implemented, and measured" (MacNeil, 2006, p. 30). Traditionally, youth development has been defined as follows:

> Youth development focuses on developmental needs and there is general recognition of two basic types: those that can be met and fulfilled, often referred to as deficit needs, and those that persist as a continuing driving force in our lives, the being needs. (Maslow & Lowery, 1998, as cited in Kress, 2006)

In recent years, the field of youth development has moved in a new direction toward youth leadership. Scholars have recognized that educators must do more than merely deposit information into the minds of students as if they are empty slates without the capacity to add value to the topic at hand. That mindset aligns with the banking concept embedded in traditional pedagogical models of education. MacNeil and McClean (2006) assert that "education is not a process of filling up learners with new information; it is a process of creating conditions that support learners in making discoveries themselves, then putting those discoveries to use" (p. 99). This has important implications for the manner in which youth leadership is developed. It has been postulated that educators who strive to develop youth leadership must adhere to the following framework:

> …we must create opportunities for young people to do more than hear stories of great leadership or participate in skills-building activities. We must work to create those contexts and relationships where young people can engage in the action of leadership, where they can practice and demonstrate leadership in an authentic and meaningful way. (pp. 99-100)

For maximum effectiveness, youth development programs need transformational leaders to empower participants to develop beyond their own expectations. This entails advanced planning to challenge youth to shift their current perspectives. Avolio (1999) stated that "the transformation my colleagues and I have studied is fundamentally about a shift in perspective, which ultimately leads to a shift in behaviors, actions, and accomplishments" (p. 207). Avolio described development as follows:

> Development in its purest sense involves the planned evolution of people's perspectives and the capacity to enlarge those perspectives to understand the needs, abilities, and aspirations of all those around you and those you will meet in the future. In this journey, your perspective will often have to continue to evolve for others around you also to advance and develop to their full potential. (p. 207)

In addition, Avolio stated the following about transformational leaders and their followers: "Your continuous personal improvement (CPI) leads to their CPIs, which in turn ignites the continuous process improvement (CPI) for the organization" (p. 207). Self-confidence and self-determination has been identified by Bass (1985) as being requisite abilities of charismatic/transformational leaders. In addition, the ability to resolve internal conflict has also been identified by Bass as a required ability to be transformational. Youth development programs in the 21st century must focus on increasing the personal leadership development of youth participants in order to yield transformative results. The Youth Citizenship Seminar was studied to better understand how 142 former participants' personal development was impacted by this transformational youth leadership development program.

The Youth Citizenship Seminar (YCS)

According to Kirnon (2008) and Musick (2008), the Southern California Youth Citizenship Seminar (YCS) was founded in 1976 by Dr. Charles B. Runnels who is a private western university's Chancellor Emeritus. These authors reported that in 1976 Dr. Runnels sensed a need to develop young leaders. Kirnon and Musick both reported that Dr. Runnels has facilitated the YCS every summer for the past 32 years in Malibu, California. The 33rd annual YCS will be held June 22, 2009 through June 26, 2009. Susan Plumb, the daughter of Dr. Runnels, is currently the director of the program.

According to Kirnon (2008) and Musick (2008), Dr. Runnels created the YCS to help students who were already demonstrating leadership skills in their schools to build on their existing talent. To that end, these authors reported that Dr. Runnels designed the YCS to reinforce student's values, to emphasize their ethics, to develop their strength in purpose, to fortify their belief in themselves as well as their belief in America and to encourage students to pave their own road to success. Kirnon reported that Dr. Runnels encourages YCS participants to dream the impossible dream. Kirnon further reported that Dr. Runnels stated that YCS will change student's lives if they allow that to happen.

Kirnon (2008) and Musick (2008) both reported that the Southern California Youth Citizenship Seminar (YCS) has counselors who volunteer to work with the participants each year. They further reported that all of the counselors in the program are former YCS participants so they have an instant connection with the current year's participants from which they can build upon throughout the week. Kirnon and Musick also stated that the YCS has approximately 25 internationally known guest speakers who volunteer to share their inspirational stories of success with the participants each year.

Kirnon and Musick stated that the guest speakers are requested to share the following information with the students: (a) who they are; (b) their journey from beginning to the present day; and (c) what being a leader means in their opinion. Their stories include obstacles they may have encountered and the ways in which they managed to overcome those obstacles. In addition to sharing their inspirational stories of success, Kirnon and Musick reported that the guest speakers interact with the YCS participants throughout the week. In addition to Dr. Runnels, the YCS counselors and the guest speakers, the YCS is facilitated by other staff members to ensure the successful implementation of the program (Kirnon; Musick).

According to Kirnon (2008) and Musick (2008), over 500 high schools in Southern California are sent a letter annually from the chancellor's office to encourage the nomination of four students in the 11th grade to participate in the Youth Citizenship Seminar (YCS). These authors reported that school principals and school counselors are responsible for nominating the students. According to Kirnon and Musick, each student who is nominated must complete an application that includes questions about his or her leadership interests. These authors further report that although the school principals and school counselors are encouraged to nominate four students to participate, only one student from each high school is selected. Sponsors of the YCS program are responsible for making the final selection. Students who are selected are those that express a strong desire to make a difference in society through their personal contribution. Approximately 250 high school juniors are selected to participate each year.

Kirnon (2008) and Musick (2008) reported that the Southern California Youth Citizenship Seminar (YCS) is a residential youth leadership program that is held every

June for five days. These authors further reported that at the time the YCS is held, each participant will have just completed the 11th grade and will be a senior in high school the following school-year. According to Kirnon and Musick, each participant is assigned to a "rap group" upon arrival and each participant remains in that rap group for the duration of the program. Each rap group consists of 15 students and one counselor. In addition to dialoging in the rap group, the YCS participants are involved in leadership activities as well as team building activities. Kirnon and Musick reported that the participants also spend time developing personal goals and sharing their life experiences with counselors and guest speakers. These authors further reported that all YCS participants and counselors reside in the private western university's dormitory during the five day program. Kirnon and Musick stated that throughout the YCS program, Dr. Runnels, the counselors and the internationally known guest speakers all emphasize the central message that everyone is equal, everyone is a leader and everyone can make a difference in the world.

Methodology

The objective of this study was to investigate how the Southern California Youth Citizenship Seminar (YCS) impacted the personal development (as outlined by Cashman, 2008) of 142 former participants who responded to a survey administered by Kirnon (2008) and Musick (2008). According to Cashman (2008):

> we are all the Chief Executive Officer's (CEO's) of our own lives: The process is the same; we lead from who we are. The leader and the person are one. As we

learn to master our growth as a person, we will be on the path to mastery of *Leadership from the Inside Out*. (p. 23)

Cashman described personal development in terms of seven practices for mastery of leadership from the inside out as follows:

These practices are not stages of development arranged in a sequential or hierarchical order. Rather, they are an ongoing, interrelated growth process in which the practices are illuminating one another. When arranged together, we can think of them as an integrated whole with each practice supporting progress toward a more fulfilling destination: making an enduring difference from within. (p. 32)

Figure 1 depicts Cashman's (2008) seven personal development practices. The first personal development practice discussed by Cashman is Personal Mastery. This practice refers to "Leading with Awareness and Authenticity" (Cashman, p. 33). Table 1 shows a comparison list of behaviors that indicate whether an individual is leading authentically from their core transformative character or from a reactive coping pattern. The second personal development practice presented is Purpose Mastery. This personal development practice refers to "Leading on Purpose" (Cashman, p. 61). Table 2 reveals the eight points for purpose mastery. The third personal development practice presented is Interpersonal Mastery. This personal development practice refers to "Leading through Synergy and Service" (Cashman, p. 79). Table 3 depicts the six points for authentic interpersonal mastery. The fourth personal development practice presented is Change Mastery. This personal development practice refers to "Leading with Agility" (Cashman,

2008, p. 105). Table 4 shows the seven change mastery shifts. The fifth personal development practice presented is Resilience Mastery. This personal development practice refers to "Leading with Energy" (p. 127).

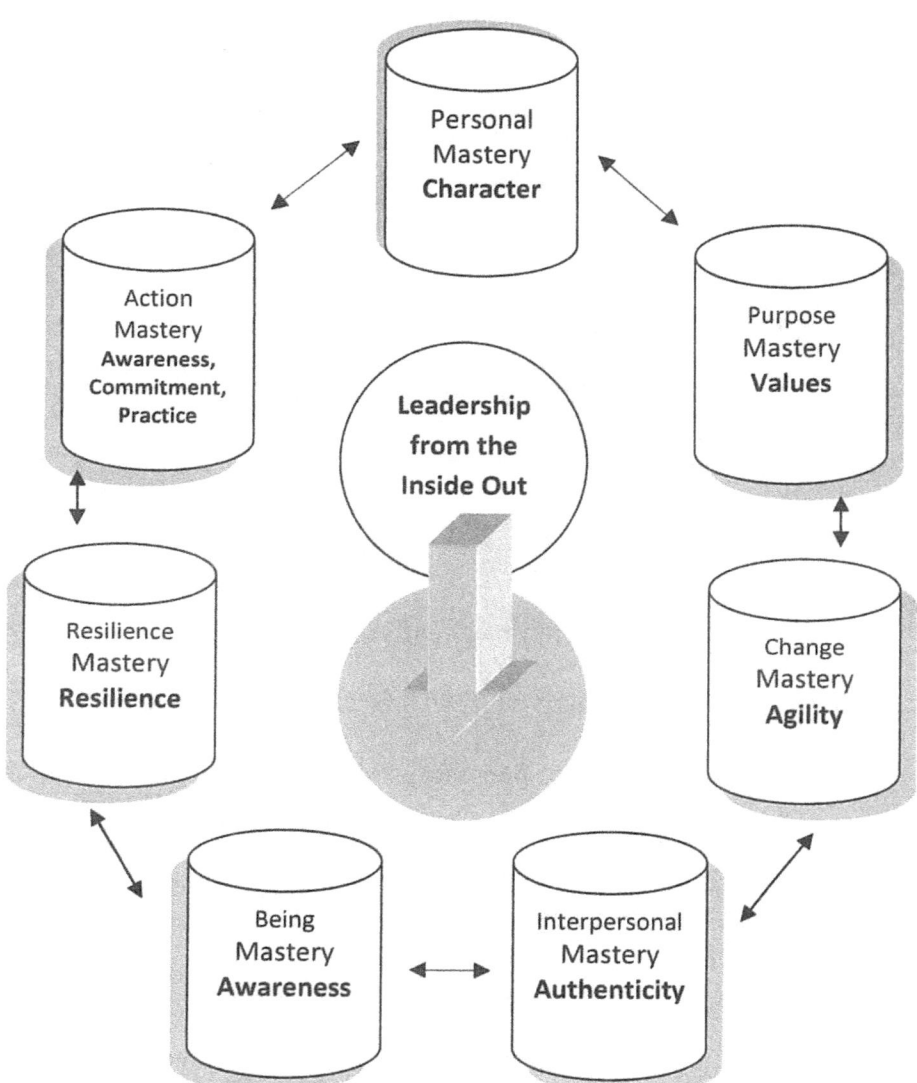

Figure 1.

Seven practices for mastery of leadership from the inside out

Table 1

Personal Mastery: Qualities of Character and Coping

CHARACTER TRANSFORMS	COPING REACTS
Opens up Possibilities and Multiplies Energy	Deals with Circumstances and Spends Energy
Guided By:	Guided By:
Authenticity	Image/Recognition
Purpose	Safety/Security/Comfort
Openness	Control
Trust	Fear
Balanced Concern for Self and Others	Concern for Self
Courage	Avoidance
Inclusion	Exclusion
Win-Win	Win-Lose
Balance/Centeredness	Anger
Agility/Resilience	Resistance to Change
Peaceful Presence	Uneasy Presence
Leader is Bigger Than Circumstance	Circumstance is Bigger Than the Leader

Table 2

Purpose Mastery: Eight Points for Purpose Mastery

1. Get in Touch with what is Important to You: Values are the guideposts to purpose. Understanding what is important, what gives meaning to our lives, is the compass to finding our purpose.
2. Act "On-Purpose": Following your dream is the most practical thing you can possibly do with your life. But you have to have commitment.
3. Find Team Core Purpose: Connect your individual purpose to the broader mission and tremendous energy and engagement will be released.
4. Do Not Mistake the Path for the Goal: Finding your purpose is finding your essence or calling in life, not just adopting the belief systems of someone else.
5. Focus on Service: Purpose always serves—it is the manner in which we use our gifts to make a difference in the world. Purpose is not purpose without adding value to others.
6. Be Purposeful in All Domains: Once you realize how your gifts can make a difference, then examine the degree to which you are being purposeful in all parts of your life.
7. Learn from "Failure": From the vantage point of Purpose Mastery, failure does not exist. It is life attempting to teach us some new lessons or trying to point some new directions.
8. Be Flexible: We need to be flexible, open to the process of expressing our internal sense of purpose in many different roles and life circumstances.

Table 3

Interpersonal Mastery: Six Points for Authentic Interpersonal Mastery

1. Know Yourself Authentically
2. Listen Authentically
3. Influence Authentically
4. Appreciate Authentically
5. Share Stories Authentically
6. Serve Authentically

Table 4

Change Mastery: Seven Change Mastery Shifts

Change Mastery Shift 1: From Problem Focus to Opportunity Focus
Change Mastery Shift 2: From Short-Term Focus to Long-Term Focus
Change Mastery Shift 3: From Circumstance Focus to Purpose Focus
Change Mastery Shift 4: From Control Focus to Agility Focus
Change Mastery Shift 5: From Self-Focus to Service
Change Mastery Shift 6: From Expertise Focus to Listening Focus
Change Mastery Shift 7: From Doubt Focus to Trust Focus

Table 5

Resilience Mastery: Eleven Points of Resilience Mastery

1. Be on Purpose, but be Aware: When we are on purpose it is most difficult for others to knock us off balance. Although we must be purposeful, we must be careful not to let our passion burn us out.
2. Foster Your Energy vs. Managing Time: Time management is a function of the clock. Energy management is the domain of leadership. It comes from within, has the capacity to increase, to go beyond what is.
3. Learning to Exercise with Ease: Instead of having the "no pain, no gain" mentality, find an activity that you love, decide to feel good about it and manage your fitness by how good you feel during and after the exercise.
4. Deal with Life-Damaging Habits: Poor lifestyle choices account for more misery, suffering, death, and imbalance in our society than any other single or multiple cause.
5. Avoid Taking Yourself So Seriously: Humor and light-heartedness energize mind, body, and spirit. The more rigid and self-centered we are, the more out of balance we become.
6. Develop Mind-Body Awareness: Most of us are stuck in our heads. We need to pay more attention to our body's messages. It is our primary feedback mechanism to revealed the positive or negative impact of our thoughts, emotions, or choices.
7. Manage Stress More Effectively: Stress is determined by how we process our world. If two people are stressed the same way, one may collapse and the other may thrive on the challenging opportunity.
8. Nurture Your Close Relationships: Close relationships can be our anchors in the sea of change. But this "closeness" does not come from others to us. It originates as intimacy with ourselves first. We can only give what we have.
9. Simplify Your Life: What are the underlying principles for simplifying life? Sort out needs vs. wants and connect with purpose.
10. Take Real Vacations: A real vacation is any time spent at home or away from home that provides you with the restorative energy and time to gain a better perspective on life.

11. Integrate More Reflection and Introspection into Your Lifestyle: Take time to reflect.

Table 5 reveals the eleven points of resilience mastery. The sixth personal development practice is Being Mastery. This personal development practice refers to "Leading with Presence" (p. 147). Table 6 shows the four points of awareness for leading with presence. The seventh and final personal development practice presented is Action Mastery. This personal development practice refers to "Leading through Coaching" (Cashman, 2008, p. 165). Table 7 depicts the three interrelated action mastery steps.

Table 6

Being Mastery: Four Points of Awareness for Leading with Presence

1. Take Your Own Journey into Being: Find your own path to unfold being. It's your road, and only you can travel it. Consider meditation, prayer, reflection, music, nature and any other "techniques" that seem to resonate with you.
2. Resolve Life Challenges by Going to a Deeper Level: Learn to go to a deeper level to view things in a more comprehensive way. As your mind learns to settle down yet remain alert, the ability to sort through and to organize your life will be amazing.
3. Consider Learning to Meditate: At least consider the possibility of learning to meditate properly. It may be the best investment in your development you ever make. If you have a particularly strong resistance to spending time with yourself in reflection or meditation, then the need to do so is probably great.
4. Integrate Some Reflection into Your Life: Getting on the path to Being involves committing to a lifestyle that values more solitude, reflection, and meditation. Take some "Being Breaks" by investing some time getting reacquainted with yourself. Enjoy the solitude. Go on some walks. Sort out your priorities. Experience the silence.

Table 7

Action Mastery: Building Awareness, Commitment and Practice

Step One: Building Awareness	Building Awareness is the process of bringing new information into our field of view. It may include keeping our attention on a newly clarified talent we have brought into focus. It may involve the more painful process of acknowledging that a behavior is unintentionally self-defeating or affecting others in a life-damaging way.
Step Two: Building Commitment	Building Commitment begins with comprehending the consequences of our actions. When we have a deep emotional connection to the impact of a behavior, our life can change permanently. It is important to recognize the consequences of any life-damaging behaviors we may have, but it is equally valuable to understand the life-enriching benefits of doing something more, less or differently.
Step Three: Building Practice	Building Practice is the process of consistently engaging in new behaviors to enrich our lives. It is the application phase of growth. While it is crucial to build awareness and to build commitment, they are not sufficient for transformation; consistent action and new, tangible pragmatic behaviors are required.

Bass (1998) recommended that future investigators should conduct research to link transformational leadership to personal development. The findings of this study added to the body of knowledge in the emerging field of youth leadership and serve as a theoretical and practical framework to guide educators in the development and implementation of effective youth programs throughout the nation. To meet the objective of this study, the following research question was developed:

How did the Southern California Youth Citizenship Seminar (YCS) impact the personal development (as described by Cashman, 2008: Personal Mastery, Purpose Mastery, Interpersonal Mastery, Change Mastery, Resilience Mastery, Being Mastery and Action Mastery) of participants who completed the Civic Involvement and Leadership survey? (Kirnon, 2008; Musick, 2008)

Research Approach and Design. The research approach used for this study was a qualitative within-site case study. According to Creswell (2007), the focus of a qualitative with-in site case study is to "develop an in-depth description and analysis of a case" (p. 78). The Southern California Youth Citizenship Seminar (YCS) was selected for this study because research conducted by both Kirnon (2008) and Musick (2008) has yielded empirical data that supports the long-term effectiveness of this youth development program. Since the Southern California YCS has had a positive impact on the lives of thousands of students since 1976, a deeper analysis of how the YCS impacted the personal development of former participants is warranted to help educators further understand the essence of their lived experience. Creswell (2007) describes this selection process as a critical case purposive sampling strategy that "permits logical generalization and maximum application of information to other cases" (p. 127).

This study was designed to investigate and describe the impact of the Southern California Youth Citizenship Seminar (YCS) on the personal development of 142 former YCS participants. An in-depth narrative analysis of the impact of the YCS program on the personal development of former participants has yielded specific information about how this program has facilitated personal development (as outlined by Cashman, 2008) in former YCS participants. Seven personal development practices for mastery of leadership from the inside out were developed and written about by Cashman. These seven mastery areas were developed to light the pathway for the growth and development of emerging leaders as well as for experienced leaders.

The following seven personal development practices were developed by Cashman (2008) and his organizational team at LeaderSource after many years of helping leaders improve their personal, team and organizational effectiveness: (a) Personal Mastery, (b) Purpose Mastery, (c) Interpersonal Mastery, (d) Change Mastery, (e) Resilience Mastery, (f) Being Mastery, and (g) Action Mastery. These seven personal development mastery areas are interrelated and together they create the pathway to the Master Competency that Cashman describes as "growing the whole person to grow the whole leader" (p. 26).

Participants. The participants in this study were 142 out of 242 former Youth Citizenship Seminar (YCS) high school students who previously participated in Kirnon (2008) and Musick's (2008) research studies. Of the original 242 former YCS participants who completed to Civic Involvement and Leadership Survey, 142 (59%)

responded to the final open ended question. This subgroup was pulled for this study because it is their responses to the final open ended question (#80) that were analyzed in this study. Within this subgroup there were 60 male participants (43%) and 81 female participants (57%). One of the respondents in this subgroup did not list his/her gender. The ages of the respondents at the time they completed the Civic Involvement and Leadership Survey ranged from 19 to 39 years old. The total number and percentage of different ethnicities represented in the subgroup who participated in this study were as follows: One (1%) American Indian or Alaska Native (1%); Two (1%) Native Hawaiian or Pacific Islander; Five (4%) Black or African American; 20 (14%) Asian; 29 (21%) Hispanic or Latino/Latina; and 93 (67%) White or Caucasian.

Participants in this study completed the Civic Involvement and Leadership Survey administered by Kirnon (2008) and Musick (2008) and submitted their responses either online or via U.S. mail. They each attended the Youth Citizenship Seminar (YCS) in Malibu, California during the 19 year period spanning from June 1997 through June 2006. Each participant had completed his/her junior year in high school before he/she arrived at YCS. All of the participants were from high schools throughout Southern California. The participants were nominated by their high school counselors or principals to attend the YCS. Although four students per school were allowed to be nominated, only one student from each high school was selected. Students who were nominated were required to submit an application that included questions about his/her leadership interests and dreams for the future. Sponsors of the YCS selected the final participants amongst all of the nominees.

Instrumentation. The Civic Involvement and Leadership Survey developed by Kirnon (2008) and Musick (2008) was the instrument used for this study. It was derived from an instrument developed by Van Horn (2001) that reflected several constructs found in research conducted by Verba and Schlozman (1995) and Youniss et al. (1997). Kirnon and Musick received van Horn's permission to use the instrument as the basis for each of their studies. Kirnon and Musick expanded Van Horn's instrument to include: (a) questions that classify each participant's level of civic engagement using the dimensions reported by Westheimer and Kahne (2004b); (b) questions specific to the YCS program; and (c) references relevant to former YCS participants.

The Civic Involvement and Leadership Survey is a questionnaire which measures the degree of civic participation and leadership development by YCS participants before, during and after the YCS program. It consists of 80 questions that yield 142 coded data elements. The questionnaire was developed to be self-administered with the majority of the questions utilizing a 5-point scale, with 1 = "never" to 5 = "always." The instrument was designed to extend van Horn's instrument by including the following constructs: (a) adult involvement and leadership in community, (b) civic and social groups, (c) political and 39 religious activities, (d) involvement as youth in community, civic/social groups, and political/religious activities, and (e) the transformational impact of YCS on each participant's civic socialization. The instrument also has questions that yield specific information about each respondent's demographic classification and socio-economic status.

The final question on the Civic Involvement and Leadership Survey (Question #80) is an open ended question that respondents can answer with either a short response or with an elaborate, detailed response. Specifically, question #80 is as follows: Please provide any further comments with respect to YCS impacting your life as a citizen and/or as a leader. The participants in this study were selected because all of them responded to question #80.

Data Collection. Data for this qualitative, with-in site case study had already been collected by Kirnon (2008) and Musick (2008). Permission to access the previously collected data was obtained and considerations given to whether subjects had been informed of possible subsequent analyses were explored. The University's Institutional Review Board (IRB) granted approval for this study as Exempt Research. The data set used consisted of 142 responses by former Southern California Youth Citizenship Seminar (YCS) participants who completed and submitted question #80 on the Civic Involvement and Leadership Survey. The specific open-ended writing prompt was as follows: (Please write) any further comments with respect to YCS impacting your life as a citizen and/or as a leader. According to Creswell (2007), documents (such as these surveys) may be used in a qualitative phenomenological inquiry for data collection. Following IRB approval, the investigator was granted access to the data which was housed in Zoomerang (http://www.zoomerang.com). The investigator read through each of the original 242 surveys and deleted all surveys that did not include a response to question #80. The investigator deleted 100 surveys that did not include responses to the final open ended question (#80). The investigator analyzed the remaining 142 responses to the following open ended writing prompt that was posed in survey question #80: Please provide any further comments with respect to YCS impacting your life as a citizen and/or as a leader. Data was compiled for analysis during the month of August 2009 which was previously collected between January 8, 2008 and February 1, 2008.

Data Processing and Analysis. A holistic analysis of the data collected was conducted by blending the six generic steps outlined by Creswell (2003) with the specific data analysis steps for this study. "An ideal situation is to blend the generic steps with the specific research design steps" (Creswell, p. 191). The data was processed and analyzed using the following six blended steps: (a) The investigator organized and prepared the program information for the Youth Citizenship Seminar (YCS) as well as the 142 survey responses for analysis; (b) The investigator read all of the information gathered about the YCS program as well as the survey responses to get an overall sense of the information; (c) The investigator organized the former participant's responses into chunks using a pre-assigned coding process derived from the seven personal development practices for mastery of leadership from the inside out framed by Cashman (2008); (d) The investigator wrote narrative descriptions about other categories that emerged; (e) The investigator wrote a narrative passage to discuss the interconnected themes that emerged from the findings of the analysis; (f) The investigator interpreted the themes that emerged, discussed the meaning of the interconnected themes and created an action agenda for youth organizations that seek to make a transformational impact in the lives of the student's they serve.

More specifically, during the first step the investigator scanned all of the data collected, sorted the data and arranged the data into different types. During the second step, the investigator read all of the data to "obtain a general sense of the information and to reflect on its overall meaning" (Creswell, 2003, p. 191). The investigator recorded notes in the data analysis section of her research journal during this step. During the third step, the investigator conducted a detailed analysis of the data using a coding process. "Coding is the process of organizing the material into 'chunks' before bringing meaning to those chunks" (Rossman & Rallis, 1998, as cited in Creswell, p. 192). A pre-assigned coding scheme derived from the seven personal development practices outlined by Cashman (2008) was used. Bogdan and Biklen (1992, as cited in Creswell, 2003) listed pre-assigned coding schemes as one type of coding system that may be used in qualitative research studies. The investigator expected more categories to emerge while organizing the data during this step in the coding process, therefore, a category for unanticipated themes was included in the coding chart (see Table 8). Although other categories did emerge, there were no unanticipated themes that emerged.

During the fourth step, the investigator went beyond identifying the themes and interconnected the themes with the seven practices for mastery of leadership from the inside out (Cashman, 2008). Creswell posited that "sophisticated qualitative studies go beyond description and theme identification and into complex theme connections" (2003, p. 194). Once the themes were identified, the investigator searched for common themes that transcended this case (Yin, 2003, as cited in Creswell, 2007). These interconnected themes are the major findings for this research study. To ensure accurate interpretation of the data, two additional researchers participated in the coding process. All three researchers read the 142 survey responses and placed them into pre-assigned categories using the coding chart on Page 22.

Table 8

Coding Chart

Pre-assigned Categories	Former YCS Participant's Survey Responses
Personal Mastery	
Purpose Mastery	
Interpersonal Mastery	
Change Mastery	
Resilience Mastery	
Being Mastery	
Action Mastery	
Unanticipated Themes	

Each coder was given a detailed description of each of the seven practices for mastery of leadership from the inside out to read and use as a reference during the coding process. Once all coders completed the coding process independently, the results were compared and discussed to validate the findings. Former YCS participant's responses were only assigned to a category if all three coders agreed upon which pre-assigned category to place each response into. Once all coders completed the coding process independently, the results were compared to ensure accurate interpretation and minimize effect of any individual biases of the researchers.

During the fifth step, the findings of the data analysis were presented in the discussion section regarding the interconnecting themes that emerged. In addition, a process model was developed and presented illustrating the interconnecting themes. During the sixth and final step, the researchers discussed the meaning of the interconnected themes and the investigator created an action agenda for youth organizations that seek to make a transformational impact in the lives of the student's they serve. Furthermore, the investigator posed new questions that arose during the data analysis phase of this research study that need to be asked in future studies that explore the relationship between transformational leadership and personal development. Data was processed and analyzed by the researchers during the months of September and October 2009.

Methodological Assumptions. The investigator assumed that the survey responses completed by former Southern California Youth Citizenship Seminar (YCS) participants were authentic, accurate and reflective of their lived experiences. The investigator also assumed that the Southern California YCS facilitated the personal development of former YCS participants in one or more of the seven personal development areas outlined by Cashman (2008).

Limitations. One of the limitations in this study is the fact that the Civic Involvement and Leadership Surveys administered by Kirnon (2008) and Musick (2008) were not completed in a controlled environment which may have had an effect on the participant's responses. Creswell (2003) noted that questionnaires are subject to considerable self-selection bias which means that former YCS participants who did not submit their questionnaire may have had a different lived experience than those who did submit their completed survey questionnaires. This may have skewed the nature and quality of the data submitted for analysis and interpretation. Another limitation inherent in studies that use qualitative data is the risk of bias influencing the interpretation. Although an accepted process for ensuring accuracy in the interpretation of qualitative data was used, results and conclusions could still be subject to different interpretations by other individuals with different perspectives.

Results

Types of Responses Written. The narratives analyzed in this study contained a variety of types of responses written by former Youth Citizenship Seminar (YCS) participants. Specifically, former participants reported the following about the YCS experience: (a) The YCS positively impacted my life in a significant manner, (b) The YCS was unforgettable, (c) The YCS made participants feel proud to have attended the program and honored to represent their high school, (d) The YCS was a great foundation for college, (e) The YCS gave participants confidence to talk to others and to take on leadership roles, (f) The YCS made participants realize that they can make a difference in their local community and in the world, (g) The YCS gave many participants a new perspective on life and helped them to grow as leaders, (h) The YCS participants were thankful for the opportunity to attend, (i) The YCS should be offered to all High School Students, (j) Some of the guest speakers were asserting their own political biases into their speeches which was not received well by the participants, and (k) The YCS experience did not impact my development. Although several respondents could recall exactly how the YCS positively impacted their growth as a citizen and as a leader, a few respondents reported that they either could not determine whether the YCS positively impacted them or they reported that the YCS did not impact them at all.

The Youth Citizenship Seminar's Impact on Personal Development. The results of this study revealed that 97% of the respondents (138 out of 142) reported that their personal development was positively impacted by participating in the Youth Citizenship Seminar (YCS). The remaining 3% of the respondents (4 out of 142) reported that their personal development was not impacted by participating in the YCS. The following sections describes how the YCS former participant's personal development was impacted according to the pre-assigned coding chart that was designed using Cashman's (2008) seven practices for mastery of leadership from the inside out.

Personal Mastery. The results of this study revealed that the second largest number of respondents (49 out of 142) reported that their personal development was positively impacted in the area of Personal Mastery. For example, one of the respondents reported that "YCS had a profound impact on my life" (YCS Participant, June, 2008). This former YCS participant continued to describe the experience of listening to one of the guest speakers:

> Right at that moment I decided to go after something I had always wanted but never thought I could achieve. That was, to become a broadcast journalist…I knew that I should shoot for the stars because as I learned, I might just hit the moon (Youth Citizenship Seminar Participant, June, 2008).

Purpose Mastery. The results of this study revealed that several of the respondents (27 out of 142) reported that their personal development was positively impacted in the area of Purpose Mastery. For example, one of the respondents reported that "Attending this program made me come to the conclusion as to what I wanted to do with my life career wise" (Youth Citizenship Seminar Participant, June, 2008).

Interpersonal Mastery. The results of this study revealed that the third largest number of the respondents (35 out of 142) reported that their personal development was positively impacted in the area of Interpersonal Mastery. For example, one of the respondents reported that "YCS was a great experience (Youth Citizenship Seminar Participant, June 2008)." This former YCS participant further noted that YCS:

> …taught me to be a better public speaker, opened my mind to new ideas and the point of views of others [sic], and lastly the people I met there were good friends some of which I kept in touch with years later. (Youth Citizenship Seminar Participant, June, 2008)

Change Mastery. The results of this study revealed that the same number of respondents that reported a positive impact in the area of interpersonal mastery (35 out of 142) reported that their personal development was positively impacted in the area of Change Mastery. For example, one of the respondents reported that "YCS helped me solidify my role as a leader and community organizer. Prior to YCS, I was hesitant to take on leadership roles but YCS gave me confidence to pursue leadership roles" (Youth Citizenship Seminar Participant, June, 2008).

Resilience Mastery. The results of this study revealed that the fifth largest number of the respondents (22 out of 142) reported that their personal development was positively impacted in the area of Resilience Mastery. For example, one of the respondents reported that "YCS was a wonderful experience that helped me become more independent and strengthened my resolve to remain actively involved in my community and in considering the interplay of societal issues" (Youth Citizenship Seminar Participant, June, 2008).

Being Mastery. The results of this study revealed that the least number of the respondents (5 out of 142) reported that their personal development was positively impacted in the area of Being Mastery. For example, one of the respondents reported the following: "I felt like YCS made me really reflect on who I am and helping me become more comfortable being in situations outside my comfort zone" (Youth Citizenship Seminar Participant, June, 2008).

Action Mastery. The results of this study revealed that the majority of the respondents (60 out of 142) reported that their personal development was positively impacted in the area of Action Mastery. For example, one of the respondents reported that "YCS was a great motivation for me. It made me realize that I could become a leader and help my community in many ways. Overall, I think YCS should keep happening so other students could attain that motivation that I did" (Youth Citizenship Seminar Participant, June, 2008).

Brief Responses. The results of this study revealed that of the 142 narrative responses, 13 of them were only one sentence in length (excluding compound sentences). The brief responses were written as follows: (a) "YCS was a catalyst in helping me realize my role as a citizen and as a leader" (Youth Citizenship Seminar Participant, June, 2008), (b) "Thanks for the opportunity to share my experience" (Youth Citizenship Seminar Participant, June, 2008), (c) "It provided a great foundation for college" (Youth Citizenship Seminar Participant, June, 2008), (d) "It was great" (Youth Citizenship Seminar Participant, June, 2008), (e) "It gave me confidence in myself to compete with other students for various positions in college" (Youth Citizenship Seminar Participant, June, 2008), (f) "Wonderful experience" (Youth Citizenship Seminar Participant, June, 2008), (g) "Opened my eyes to new things" (Youth Citizenship Seminar Participant, June, 2008), (h) "The motivational speakers had the most lasting effect" (Youth Citizenship Seminar Participant, June, 2008), (i) "I am still thankful for the wonderful opportunity to attend YCS" (Youth Citizenship Seminar Participant, June, 2008), (j) "It was AMAZING, truly…" (Youth Citizenship Seminar Participant, June, 2008), (k) "Positive growth experience, overall" (Youth Citizenship Seminar Participant, June, 2008), (l) "I do not remember it being that important in my development" (Youth Citizenship Seminar Participant, June, 2008), (m) "It was a wonderful experience that encouraged my dedication to community service and outreach" (Youth Citizenship Seminar Participant, June, 2008).

Detailed Responses. The results of this study revealed that of the 142 narrative responses, 41 of them were one paragraph in length or longer. The most detailed of the narrative responses is as follows:

> It was at YCS that I first spoke with a real defense attorney and got a sense of what that life was like (I forgot his name but he routinely did the last speech for the whole crowd). Even though I didn't know it then, that impression would guide me towards what I wanted to do later. Beyond that, YCS really got me out of my little corner of the world… and exposed me to equally driven students from throughout the state. I saw a similar level of diversity and drive when I started law school. I don't think YCS necessarily answered any questions for me in a definitive form. Rather, it was a week of really positive collective focus that opened me up to new answers and new possibilities. I thought it was a wonderful program then and now. Finally, my sense of service was profoundly altered by that defense attorney. He was one of the first people to really point out to me that service is not about a label (head of this club, chief donator, etc...) or recognition. Rather, service is seeing a potential to help, and just doing it, whether that is coaching the local football team, debate team, or just stopping to help a stranger who is pushing their broken down car up the road and out of the street. In college, I would often quote and think about this statement from Martin Luther King, Jr.: "Anyone can be great, because anyone can serve." When I first heard

that quotation, I thought about that concept of helping to help, not just because of appearance. YCS both exposed me to this kind of greatness and it is an example of it. Thanks for helping me, and I am grateful you continue to help others.
(Youth Citizenship Seminar Participant, June, 2008)

Discussion

The Youth Citizenship Seminar. After reading literature about the Youth Citizenship Seminar (YCS), perusing their website and attending the week-long seminar for all five days during the June 2009 session, I gained a deeper awareness of exactly how empowering and how significantly impactful the YCS actually can be for participants. Just as the Director of the program, Susan Plumb, promised in her letter written in the spiral-bound notebook given to each of the participants before the YCS began, the world renowned guest speakers made the magic of the YCS come to life. Each speaker shared inspirational stories of success that authentically displayed their self-confidence and their determination. This type of presentation demonstrates to each participant how important self-confidence and determination is to reaching goals. These two qualities, self-confidence and determination, are requisites to transformational leadership (Bass, 1985). Hence, personal development in the areas of self-confidence and determination will not only help youth participants reach their goals but will also assist them towards becoming transformational leaders themselves.

The magic of the YCS is based upon Dr. Runnel's personal secret to success that he calls the five points of light: (a) Vision, (b) Integrity, (c) Courage, (d) Education, and (e) Service. The acronym for the five points of light was written on the lanyards worn by all of the YCS counselors and staff members (V.I.C.E.S.). This acronym was frequently referred to during the YCS by the guest speakers as well as by the counselors during rap sessions or during general sessions between speakers.

Transformational Leadership. The guest speakers who speak at the Youth Citizenship Seminar (YCS) all demonstrate a transformational leadership style. They are charismatic, inspirational leaders who tailor their messages to youth with great consideration given to what they need at this stage in their adolescent development. In addition, through the power of their own testimony they deliver speeches that intellectually stimulate the YCS participants. Similarly, the YCS counselors are authentic leaders who take the time to get to know the participants which makes it easy for them to know what their followers needs are. Since transformational leaders can best meet their followers needs when they get to know them, authenticity is imperative to allow the followers to gain trust in the leaders and open up to them.

Other components of the Youth Citizenship Seminar (YCS) demonstrate the transformational nature of the program. For example, the talent show gives each participant the opportunity to display his/her talent. By giving the participants an opportunity to discover and display their talents, this demonstrates individual consideration by the YCS program administrators. Another example of the transformational nature of the YCS involves the rap sessions. The rap sessions were designed and included as a component of the program to intellectually stimulate the YCS participants and pique their interest in becoming actively involved in community issues that they are passionate about. This component of the YCS gives the participants an opportunity for personal development in the area of Action Mastery which includes three interrelated action mastery steps: awareness, commitment and practice (Cashman, 2008).

Transformational Leadership and Personal Development. The results of this study revealed that transformational leadership is positively correlated with increased personal development. In the case of the Youth Citizenship Seminar (YCS), the use of a transformational leadership style coupled with the five points of light as the core personal development curriculum, gives the participants of the YCS an opportunity for personal development in all seven mastery areas. The YCS utilizes the five points of light: (a) Vision, (b) Integrity, (c) Courage, (d) Education, and (e) Service as the core of their personal development curriculum which gives each YCS participant the opportunity for personal development during each of the components of the program. The transformational leadership style of the YCS along with their well-rounded personal development curriculum creates the necessary framework to produce transformative outcomes for youth participants.

All of the components of the YCS are designed to help each participant understand that he or she needs to dream the impossible dream (Vision), to live by his/her personal values (Integrity), to not be afraid of challenging situations (Courage), to develop academically (Education) and to be actively involved in their schools and community (Service). Many of the students who participate in the YCS have already been inspired to follow their dreams and to be actively involved in their community and the majority of the respondents received further inspiration during this program. As a doctoral student, having received lots of inspiration from my parents (like the former YCS participants), I was also inspired during my attendance of the June 2009 YCS as an observer. With that in mind, I believe that the positive impact of the YCS and similar transformational youth leadership development programs would prove to be even more impactful to a population of youth who have not received such inspiration from their parents or another adult role model.

Seven Areas of Personal Development. This study revealed that Action Mastery was the area of personal leadership where the majority (60 out of 142) of former Youth Citizenship Seminar (YCS) Participants reported a positive impact as a citizen and as a leader. According to the respondents' narratives, personal development in this area involved these youth participants building an awareness of new information and perspectives, building a commitment to change any life-damaging behaviors being demonstrated and building practice with engaging in newly learned behaviors that enriched their lives. Personal development in this area has proven to be life-changing for former YCS participants and was evident in close to half of the respondents in this study.

Personal Mastery was the area of personal development where the second largest number of respondents (49 out of 142) reported a positive impact on their lives as a citizen and as a leader. According to the respondents' narratives, personal development in this area involved these youth participants opening their minds to new possibilities and transforming their character by building their courage, developing their understanding that they need to live with a specific purpose in mind, increasing their level of authenticity and having a balanced concern for themselves and others. Personal development in the area or Personal Mastery has helped to build the respondents' requisite characteristics of transformational leaders which include self-confidence and determination (Bass, 1985).

Interpersonal Mastery and Change Mastery were the two areas of personal development where an equal number of respondents (35 out of 142) reported a positive impact on their lives as a citizen and as a leader. According to the respondents' narratives, personal development in the area of Interpersonal Mastery involved these youth participants learning more about their who they are, learning how to listen to others with an open mind, learning how to influence others by sharing their own testimonies and learning how to serve others the only intention of making a difference other people's lives (as opposed to serving in order to receive recognition for service). In the area of Change Mastery, respondents reported that personal development in this area included shifting their focus from doubt to trust (regarding their individual ability) and shifting their focus from self towards service. Personal development in the area of Interpersonal Mastery has helped to build these youth participants' ability to interact and socialize with others while personal development in the area of Change Mastery has helped to build their confidence and helped to develop their deep desire to serve others.

Purpose Mastery was an area of personal development where approximately 1/5 of the respondents (27 out of 142) reported a positive impact on their lives as a citizen and as a leader. According to these respondents' narratives, personal development in the area of Purpose Mastery involved helping these youth participants realize what is important to them, helping them to decide to follow their dreams and helping them to connect their individual purpose with a broader mission to make a greater positive impact in the world.

Personal development in the area of Purpose Mastery helped to build these youth participants' awareness of their values and helped them to clarify which career path they should follow.

Resilience Mastery was an area of personal development where the second lowest number of respondents (22 out of 142) reported a positive impact on their lives as a citizen and as a leader. According to these respondents' narratives, personal development in the area of Resilience Mastery involved helping these youth participants nurture close relationships, helping them to simplify life by focusing on what is important to them and helping them to look introspectively at themselves leading them to lifestyles that were more closely aligned with their purpose. Personal development in the area of Resilience Mastery has helped these youth participants' ground themselves firmly in their purpose which made them better equipped to overcome obstacles and refocus following a setback.

Although the least amount of respondents (5 out of 142) reported that the Youth Citizenship Seminar (YCS) positively impacted them in the area of Being Mastery (reflection), this area of personal development has been woven into the program. Since the YCS is a residential program, the participants have built in time for reflection each night in their dorm rooms while they are away from home. The residential nature of the program gives the participants an opportunity for personal development in the area of Being Mastery. In addition to this built in time of reflection each night, participants also have the opportunity to reflect upon their lives as they hear each guest speaker, participate in rap sessions, participate in the talent show and interact with new peers.

Interconnected Themes. The results of this study revealed that 17 out of 142 respondents reported that their personal development was positively impacted in all seven areas of personal development as outlined by Cashman (2008). As the investigator and the two coders read each of the 142 responses and re-read the descriptions for each of the seven interrelated personal development practices for mastery of leadership from the inside out, we gained a deeper understanding of the interrelated nature of these seven practices as described by Cashman. These seven personal development practices are:

> …an ongoing, interrelated growth process in which the practices are illuminating one another. When arranged together, we can think of them as an integrated whole with each practice supporting progress toward a more fulfilling destination: making an enduring difference from within. (p. 32)

The primary investigator in this study as well as the two data analysis coders all agree that using Cashman's (2008) operational definition, all positive impact statements reported by former YCS participants that fit in at least one personal development area actually illuminated the other areas as a byproduct. Thus, as growth occurs in one area of personal development, other areas will inadvertently grow as well. Although only 17 out of the 142 respondents wrote their responses in a manner that captured the positive impact of the Youth Citizenship Seminar on their personal development in all seven areas of personal development, the nature of Cashman's description of these seven practices leads this investigator to believe that the 97% of respondents whose personal development was positively impacted by attending YCS also experienced growth in all areas of personal development. The open ended nature of the survey question did not give the respondents the opportunity to fully describe the impact YCS had on their personal development as described by Cashman.

The Youth Citizenship Seminar (YCS) has seven components and each of these components has the five points of light at its core. The seven components include the following: (a) Guest speakers, (b) Counselors, (c) New friends (Fellow participants), (d) The five points of light: Vision, Integrity, Courage, Education and Service (V.I.C.E.S); (e) Seminar Topics, (f) Rap group meetings, and (g) The Pepperdine University Campus. The seven components of the (YCS) are interrelated much like the seven areas of personal development as defined by Cashman (2008). As shown in Figure 2, the seven components of YCS are interrelated by way of the five points of light.

Themes Transcending This Case. Two themes emerged that transcend this case study as follows: (a) A wide range of impact on former Youth Citizenship Seminar (YCS) participants; and (b) The majority of the respondent's impact statements were positive. The range of impact was reported by the respondents in this study as follows: No impact to minimal impact to a life-changing impact (see Figure 3). In light of the fact that the YCS yielded such positive results from the majority of former participants, youth leadership programs that aim to increase participant's personal development are likely to yield a similar pattern of impact with different populations (ex. Students demonstrating low academic achievement or students who have not demonstrated leadership skills yet).

Cassel (2003) conducted a comparison study between 1005 incarcerated juvenile delinquents and adult prison inmates and a corresponding group of typical individuals by

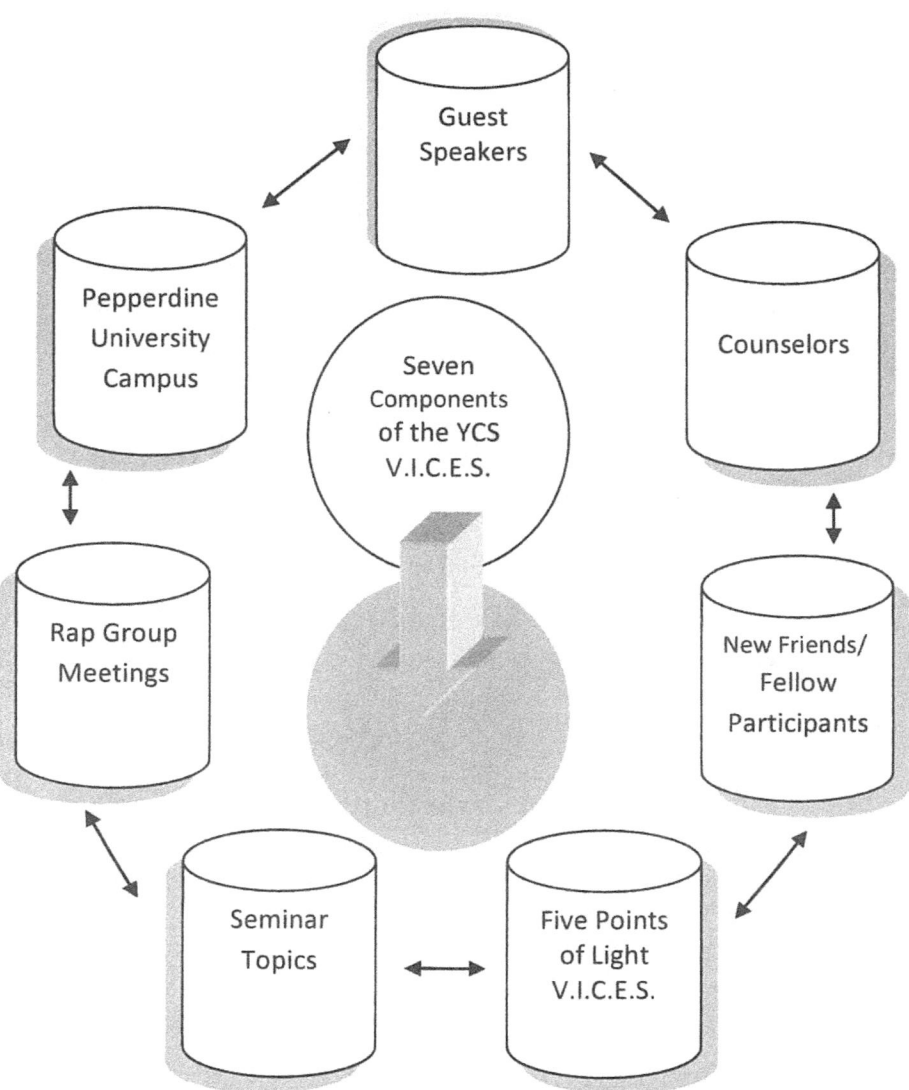

Figure 2.

Interrelated components of the youth citizenship seminar

administering a personal development test. Every score on the tests revealed significantly lower personal development for the inmates and the juvenile delinquents. Based on this data, Cassel suggested that students who face academic and/or social challenges should participate in a personal development program to prevent them from dropping out of high school.

Conclusions

The findings in this study revealed a positive relationship between the use of a transformational leadership style and increased personal development. The respondents in this study reported a wide range of impact from life changing to no impact (see Figure 3). The greatest number of respondents reported a positive impact in their personal development in the area of Action Mastery. This finding indicates that youth leadership programs that utilize a transformational leadership style plus a comprehensive personal development curriculum are likely to produce transformative outcomes in the majority of the students in their programs (see Figure 4). Educators who implement transformational youth leadership development programs will be more likely to yield a life-changing impact in the lives of the youth who participate in their programs as opposed to youth leadership programs that incorporate a transactional leadership style that lacks a comprehensive personal development curriculum.

There were several types of responses captured in the written narratives which revealed that the Youth Citizenship Seminar (YCS) impacted the former participants in a variety of ways. While the majority of the respondents reported that the YCS had a

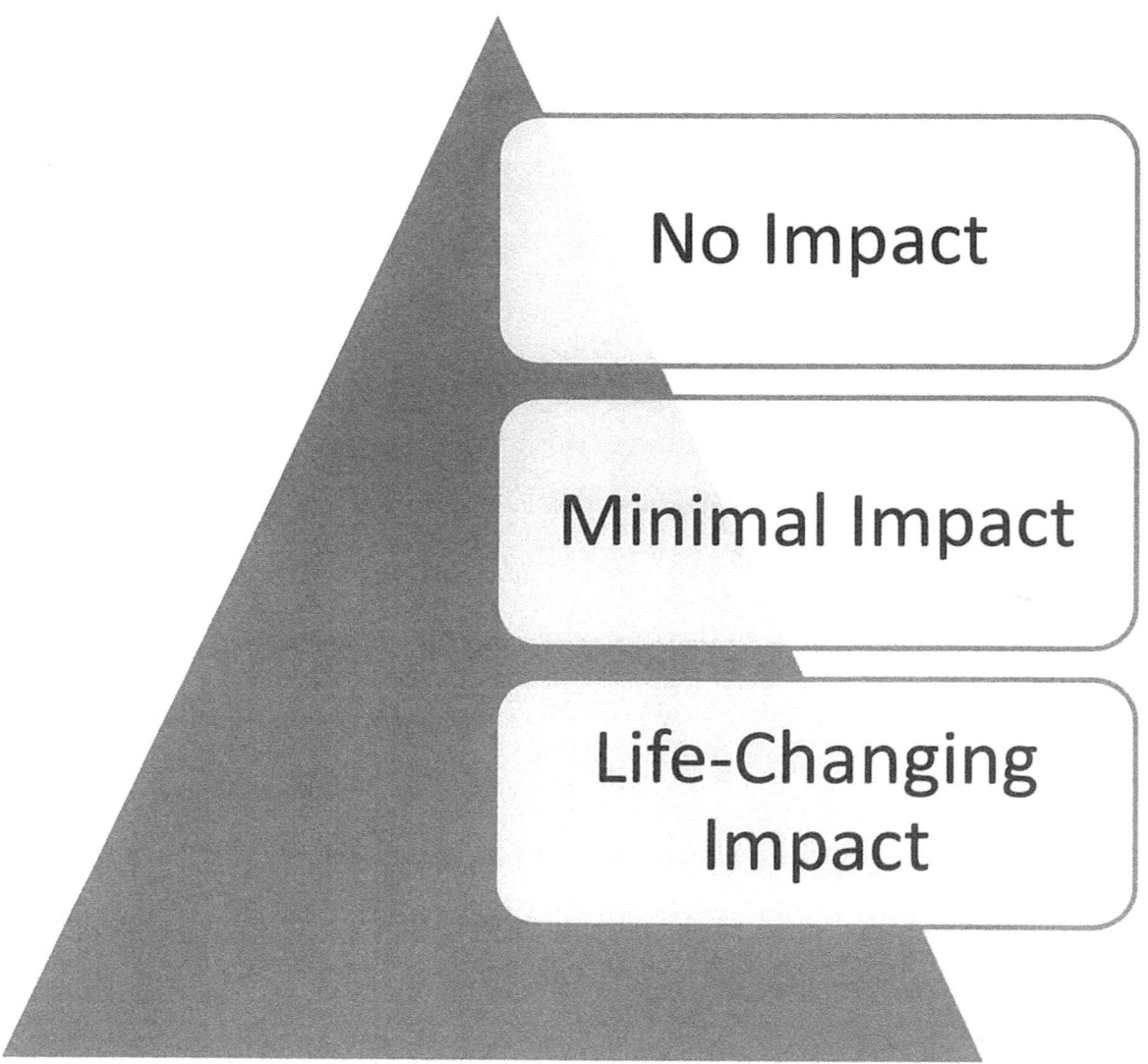

Figure 3.

Transformational Youth Leadership Programs: Range of Impact

significantly positive impact on their lives as a citizen or a leader, a few respondents reported that they were not impacted at all. Since the survey question was open-ended and the specific nature of the responses was unsolicited, the large number of positive, detailed responses further indicates that the YCS did have a positive impact on the majority of the participants.

In addition, a small set of respondents reported that many of the guest speakers were presenting their "political propaganda" and expressed their discontent at the "blatant political biases." One of the respondents reported that he was turned off by one of the speakers because the respondent had prior knowledge that this particular speaker had supported a cause that he did not believe in (Youth Citizenship Seminar Participant, June, 2008). This comment illuminates the importance for the adolescent population to hear opposing views from speakers that represent the full political spectrum. In a democratic society, it is important for our youth to understand that it is common for individuals to have different opinions and perspectives regarding societal issues.

Hearing stories that incorporate opposing views from a wide variety of leaders will encourage our youth and support them as they develop and begin to understand that there are multiple perspectives which one needs to respect. A balanced presentation of different perspectives on different issues will also help adolescents firmly develop their own perspectives on key societal issues.

A couple of the respondents commented in their narratives about the fact that the population of youth who participated in the Youth Citizenship Seminar (YCS) only included the type of high school students who "are already leaders" and "who already had privileges and experiences that ensured their success" (Youth Citizenship Seminar Participant, June, 2008). One respondent elaborated by exclaiming that "I felt like it was

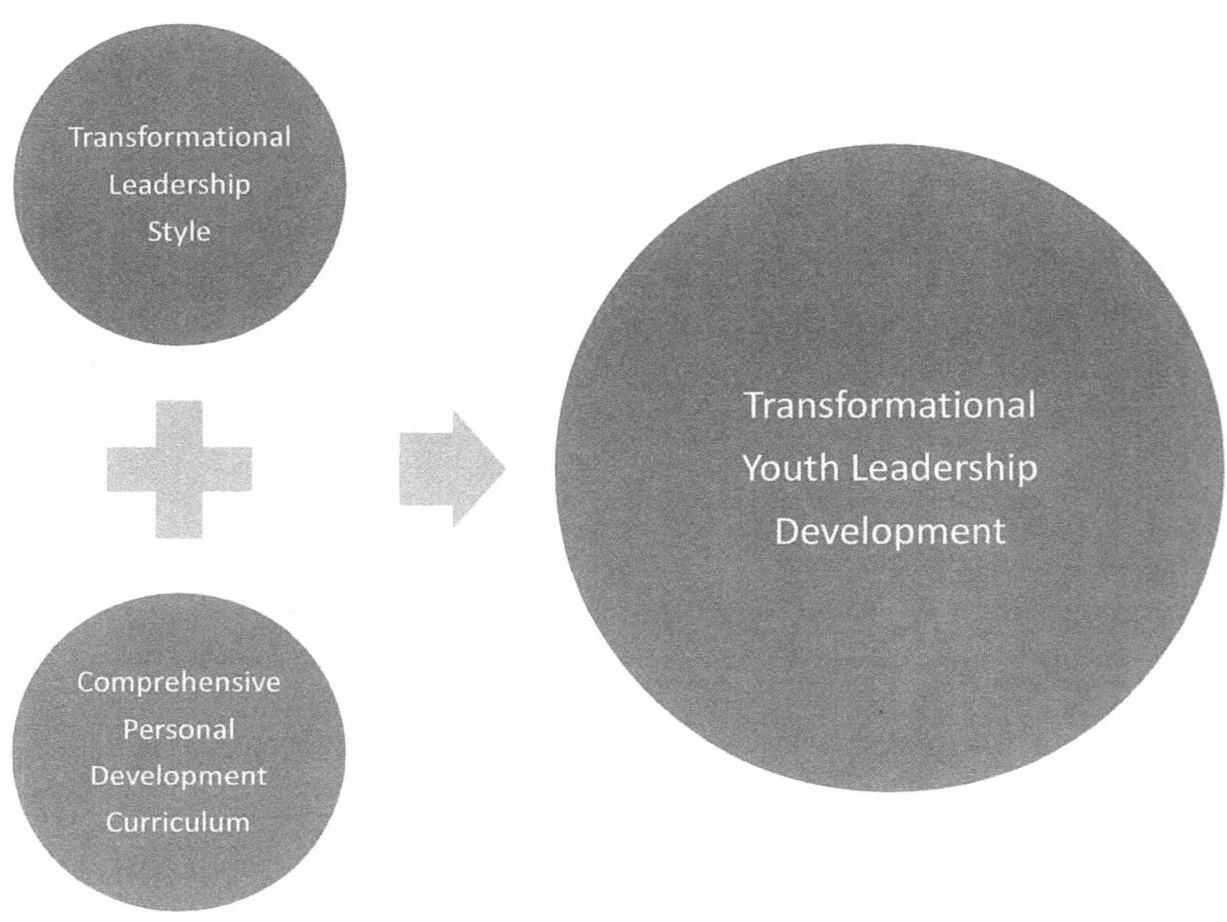

Figure 4.

Vital components of transformational youth leadership programs

not geared towards inclusion with low income diverse people" (Youth Citizenship Seminar Participant, June, 2008). The Youth Citizenship Seminar (YCS) was indeed founded with the intention of further developing the leadership skills of high school students who were already demonstrating leadership in their schools and communities, however, students who have not yet begun to demonstrate leadership skills could benefit from an opportunity to experience an empowering program such as the YCS. Also the sampling procedure used by the YCS does not include schools with a high population of diverse students which constitutes the reason for a lack of diversity amongst youth participants. A purposive sampling procedure that includes a balanced number of high schools with a diverse population along with high schools with a predominately Caucasian population would increase the pool of diverse student leaders being nominated to the program. Furthermore, when student leaders are selected to participate by the sponsors of the program, the number of students chosen from each of the schools represented would need to be monitored. Since the sample used in this study does not include an equally diverse representation of different ethnicities or socio-economic groups, the findings in this study may have been skewed. For example, a greater impact may have been reported in the area of Resilience Mastery if the sample included more high school students who have had to manage stress associated with poverty, crime-stricken neighborhoods, emotional trauma, unsafe schools or an unstable home life.

One of the respondents reported that he/she wished that someone affiliated with the Youth Citizenship Seminar (YCS) had contacted him/her for an earlier follow up (Youth Citizenship Seminar Participant, June, 2008). This respondent felt that a more immediate response to the YCS experience would have helped him/her to understand the type of immediate impact YCS had on him/her as a senior in high school (Youth Citizenship Seminar Participant, June, 2008). This implies that summative evaluations given at the conclusion of the transformational youth leadership development program and periodically thereafter are likely to yield more information about the impact of a particular youth program. These evaluations would not only be useful to the program administrators but insightful for the youth participants. In addition, formative evaluations given to participants throughout the program is another component that would add depth to the information collected regarding the impact of a transformational youth leadership development program.

Since the respondents in this study were required to answer an open ended question about the impact of the YCS on them as a citizen and as a leader, they were able to use their discretion as to how they chose to respond to the question. Therefore, while several of the respondents' narratives were a paragraph or more in length, several other narratives were only one sentence in length. Subsequently, several of the responses were not elaborate enough to capture the comprehensive manner in which their lives were actually impacted. This implies that there may have been even a greater number of respondents who were positively impacted in each of the seven areas of personal development. Furthermore, the fewest number of responses were placed in the area of being mastery. While this may be attributed to the open-ended nature of the survey question, it also may be indicative of the fact that the participants were in the middle of adolescence when they participated in the YCS and during adolescence little reflection and introspection is done. The fact that five responses were coded in the area of being mastery indicates that the YCS did in fact encourage reflection.

Burns (1978) explained that, "one of the most serious failures in the study of leadership has been the bifurcation between the literature on leadership and the literature on followership" (p. 3). Since the late 70's when Burns made that statement, research has been conducted to bring the bodies of literature on leadership together with the literature on followership. Educators and researchers are faced with a new challenge in the 21st century. The challenge stems from the fact that although research in the field of youth leadership development has recently emerged, there continues to be a bifurcation between the literature on adult leadership theories and the literature on youth development. The transformational leadership theories and the personal leadership development constructs used in this study as a framework for analyzing the Youth Citizenship Seminar (YCS) were both originally developed based on research conducted on adults. The transformative results revealed in this study indicate that the transformational leadership theories and the personal leadership development constructs developed based on historical research conducted on adults also apply to the adolescent population.

Recommendations

In order to obtain a more representative sample of youth leaders to participate in the Youth Citizenship Seminar (YCS), the administrators of the YCS should consider using a sampling procedure that includes recruiting high school students from high schools that are located in lower socio-economic areas. Furthermore, In addition to the counselors and administrators selecting participants, the selection process should include the perspectives of the students by allowing student leaders to submit their own name or a peers' name as a nominee to attend the YCS.

Since several respondents reported that the Youth Citizenship Seminar (YCS) was a great introduction to the college life and many of them later decided to attend the university where the YCS was hosted, other private universities and state universities should consider hosting residential leadership camps. Universities should consider hosting residential leadership camps for two reasons: (a) To give more high school students the opportunity to experience a potentially life-changing event; (b) To introduce more high school students to their campus which increases the likelihood that some of these students will enroll in their college.

Educators in public schools, private schools and other youth serving organizations who aim to design youth programs that produce transformative results should consider using the following action agenda: (a) Interview and hire staff who have a transformational leadership style because when transformational leaders model their leadership style it is oftentimes reciprocated by their followers (Bass, 1985); (b) Design your youth leadership development curriculum to include lessons and activities targeting each of the seven personal development practices for mastery of leadership from the inside out (Cashman, 2008); (c) Implement a curriculum training program before the starting date of the youth leadership program to effectively teach the staff how the components of the personal development curriculum should be delivered to youth participants; (d) Conduct formative and summative evaluations of the youth leadership development program to measure the transformative outcomes as reported by the youth participants. Transformational youth leadership development programs are of great value in our society and play a vital role in helping adolescents develop the foundational personal leadership skills necessary for leading an effective and productive life. These foundational personal leadership skills include the requisite skills for future transformational leaders. Accordingly, it is critical for every youth leadership development program to utilize a curriculum with lessons and activities designed to develop the following requisite skills for transformational leadership: Self-Confidence, Self-Determination and the ability to resolve internal conflict (Bass).

Future studies on transformational leadership should utilize a questionnaire that has specific questions about each of the four I's associated with transformational leadership: (a) Idealized influence which was originally referred to as charisma by Bass (1985), (b) Inspirational leadership, (c) Individualized consideration, and (d) Intellectual Stimulation (Bass & Avolio, 1993). Future studies on transformational leadership should also utilize a questionnaire based on the characteristics of transformational leaders (Tichy & Devanna, 1986). Moreover, future studies on personal development should utilize a questionnaire that has specific questions about each of the seven practices for mastery of leadership from the inside out (Cashman, 2008) in an effort to gain more precise information about the impact of the youth leadership development program as it relates more closely to each of the seven areas of personal development.

Specific questions to be asked in future studies about transformation leadership and personal development include the following: (a) How has your participation in this youth leadership development program impacted your self-confidence?; (b) How has your participation in this youth leadership development program impacted your self-determination?; (c) Has your participation in this youth leadership development program opened your mind to new possibilities about your future (Personal Mastery)? If yes, please explain how; (d) How has your participation in this youth leadership development program impacted your knowledge of what you value (Purpose Mastery)?; (e) How has your participation in this youth leadership development program impacted your ability to listen to and influence others (Interpersonal Mastery)?; (f) How has your participation in this youth leadership development program impacted your ability to focus on service to others (Change Mastery)?; (g) How has your participation in this youth leadership development program impacted your ability to manage stress more effectively (Resilience Mastery)?; (h) How has your participation in this youth leadership development program impacted your ability to reflect upon and look introspectively into your life (Being Mastery)?; (i) Has your participation in this youth leadership development program impacted your ability stop engaging in life-damaging behaviors and engage in more productive/enriching behaviors? If yes, explain how (Action Mastery). Questions one and two will yield specific information about how a youth leadership development program has developed the requisite behaviors needed for a transformational leadership style to be acquired. Moreover, questions three through nine will yield specific information about how a youth leadership program has impacted the personal development of youth participants in each of the seven areas of mastery of leadership from the inside out.

REFERENCES

Ancess, J. (2003). *Beating the odds: High schools as communities of commitment.* New York, NY: Teachers College Press.

Avolio, B. J. (1999). *Full leadership development: Building the vital forces in organizations.* Thousand Oaks, CA: Sage.

Bass, B. M. (1985). *Leadership and performance beyond expectations.* New York, NY: Free Press.

Bass, B. M., & Avolio, B. J. (1993). Transformational leadership and organizational culture. *Public Administration Quarterly, 17*(1), 112-121.

Bennis, W. G., & Nanus, B. (1985). *Leaders: The strategies for taking charge.* New York, NY: Harper & Row.

Burns, J. M. (1978). *Leadership.* New York, NY: Harper & Row.

Cashman, K. (2008). *Leadership from the inside out: Becoming a leader for life.* San Francisco, CA: Berrett-Koehler.

Cassel, R. (2003). *A high school drop-out prevention program for the at-risk sophomore students.* Chula Vista, CA: The Cassel Research Institute.

Civic Involvement and Leadership Survey. (N.D.) Retrieved January 24, 2011, from http://www.zoomerang.com

Creswell, J. W. (2003). *Research design: Qualitative, quantitative and mixed methods approaches.* Thousand Oaks, CA: Sage.

Creswell, J. W. (2007). *Qualitative inquiry and research design: Choosing among five approaches.* Thousand Oaks, CA: Sage.

Downtown, J. V. (1973). *Rebel leadership: Commitment and charisma in a revolutionary process.* New York, NY: Free Press.

Kegan, R. (1982). The *evolving self: Problem and process in human development*. Cambridge, MA: Harvard University Press.

Kirnon, S. (2008). *Inspiring citizenship and leadership: Youth citizenship seminar*. Malibu, CA: Pepperdine University.

Kress, C. (2006). Youth leadership and youth development: Connections and questions. *New directions for youth development: Youth leadership, 109*, 45-56.

Kuhnert, K. W., & Lewis, P. (1987). Transactional and transformational leadership: A constructive/developmental analysis. *Academy of Management Review, 12*(4), 648-657.

Larson, S. (2005). Teaching for transformation in today's challenging youth. *Reclaiming Children and Youth, 14*(1), 27-31.

Libby, M., Sedonaen, M., and Bliss, S. (2006). The mystery of youth leadership development: The path to just communities. *New directions for youth development: Youth leadership, 109*, 13-25.

MacNeil, C. (2006). Bridging generations: Applying "adult" leadership theories to youth leadership development. *New directions for youth development: Youth leadership, 109*, 27-43.

MacNeil, C., and McClean, J. (2006). Moving from "youth leadership development" to "youth in governance": Learning leadership by doing leadership. *New directions for youth development: Youth leadership, 109*, 99-106.

Matsudaira, J. (2006). Anytown: NCCJ's Youth Leadership Experience in Social Justice. *New directions for youth development: Youth leadership, 109*, 107-115.

Mitroff, I. (1978). Systemic problem solving. In M. W. McCall & M. M. Lombardo (Eds.), *Where else can we go?* (pp. 129-143). Durham, NC: Duke University Press.

Musick, M. (2008). *Socializing youth for adult citizenship roles: The youth citizenship seminar*. Malibu, CA: Pepperdine University.

Northouse, P. G. (2004). *Leadership: Theory and practice* (3rd ed.). Thousand Oaks, CA: Sage.

Ruget, V. (2006). The renewal of civic education in France and in America: Comparative perspectives. *Social Science Journal*, 43(1), 19-34.

Soumerai, E. & Mazer, R. (2006). Arts-based leadership: Theatrical tributes. *New directions for youth development: Youth leadership, 109*, 117-124.

Tichy, N. M., & Devanna, M. A. (1986). *The transformational leader*: New York, NY: John Wiley.

Van Horn, B. E. (2001). *Youth, family and club experiences and adult civic engagement*. University Park, PA: The Pennsylvania State University.

Verba, S., & Schlozman, K. L. (1995). *Voice and equality: Civic volunteerism in American politics*. Cambridge, MA: Harvard University Press.

Westheimer, J., & Kahne, J. (2004b). What kind of citizen? The politics of educating for democracy. *American Educational Research Journal, 41*(2), 237-269.

Wheeler, W. & Edlebeck, C. (2006). Leading, learning, and unleashing potential: Youth leadership and civic engagement. *New directions for youth development: Youth leadership, 109*, 89-97.

Youniss, J., McLellan, J. A., & Yates, M. (1997). What we know about engendering civic identity. *The American Behavioral Scientist, 40*(5), 620-631.

Youth Citizenship Seminar (YCS) information. (2009). Retrieved May 5, 2009, from http://pepperdineycs.com

Zacharatos, A., & Barling, J. (2000). Development and effects of transformational leadership in adolescents. *Leadership Quarterly, 11*(2), 211-226.

www.ingramcontent.com/pod-product-compliance
Lightning Source LLC
Chambersburg PA
CBHW080527110426
42742CB00017B/3266